I0213725

Wind

POEMS BY

TIM 2 TAYLOR

TAYLOR PRODUCTIONS

JACKSONVILLE

Copyright © 2016 by Tim Taylor Productions, Inc. All rights reserved.
This book in print, in digital e-publication, or audio or video formats may not
be copied or published in whole or in part without the prior written permission
of the author.

Copyright ©2016 by Tim Taylor

Wind - New Poems
First Printed Edition - 2016
First Digital Edition - 2016

Published by Tim Taylor Productions, Inc.
7536 Pottsburg Landing Drive
Jacksonville, Florida 32216

www.thefoundpoet.com
tim2taylor@facebook.com
#tim2taylor

Written by Tim 2 Taylor
Designed by Tim 2 Taylor
Edited by Tim 2 Taylor
Cover photography by Tim 2 Taylor

Library of Congress Control Number -

Taylor, Timothy, 1960 -

Manufactured in the United States
ISBN - 978-0-9833382-9-1 (book)
ISBN - 978-0-9833382-8-4 (e-book)

Printed copies by
Lightning Source Inc.
14 Ingram Blvd.
La Vergne, TN USA 37086
1. Poetry
Distributed by Tim Taylor Productions, Inc.
To purchase copies in bulk please contact: (904)-238-0889

To book Tim 2 Taylor for personal appearances, book signings or motivational
speaking engagements, please call (904) 238-0889 or contact Tim 2 through
the website at www.thefoundpoet.com

Be sure to read my other books: *The Found Poet- winter and The Found Poet- summer*
Look for my weight-loss and fitness book *Fat As My Dad*
Watch for my new book "Life Loops™"

"And forget not
that the earth delights
to feel your bare feet
and the winds long
to play with your hair"

– Kahlil Gibran
   The Prophet

CONTENTS

PREFACE

Writing often overtakes me. In the mornings in bed, or in my
garden, or under the moonlight. It comes blowing thought me.
The ether of inspiration is inhaled, from where it comes I believe
is the breath of God.

    This book is titled "Wind" for these days I feel the winds more
distinctly. Like a old sailor, I'm ever perceiving her direction and
power to set my course.

    I've witnessed how all of nature harvests her. Birds and leaves,
butterfly and bees all hold her close. Horses who listen to her stories
and hawks that screech her glories.

    As a young man I stood against the wind, don't we all blistery.
Alas with time, I've learned to live within her comely flow.
This is the secret of coming to love the heart of the wind.
I hope you enjoy my words.

Namaste

Tim 2 Taylor

Oh Swimming

Will you
dance around
the stars

break through
the clouds
sparkling soft

will your dress
fall tender
to the ground

sprinting towards
rolling waters
warm night

splash beneath
the waves
shimmering
laugher

swimming
swimming
oh swimming

in the dark
with a thousand candles
in my divine sea

New moonshine

When did I last
venture out
into the mystical night
to feel the soft magic
of new moonshine

brewed raw at sunset
distilled orange
lowly rising huge
clear and warm

burning buttery
over the tree line
Luna called my name
sweetly come
come from your resting dust

for when was it last
I howled in the night
and wondered
slowly
in the silvery woods

to sneak out an open window
to partake in a silly
clandestine activity
under the cover
of darkened night

skin shivering fire
the touch of her
held in the arms of the night
to kiss dizzy out beneath
new moonshine

With grander wings

I found a bird
without air
laying still upon this earth

my heart saddened
for missing his clear song
and his blue sky ways

I can't help but to question
feeling the aching depth
and pouring tears

still, solemnly
I take heart
from the knowing

and within me
I can rejoice
with assurance in peace

that this day he sings
a new song under a new sky
with grander wings

Amen

Your cup

Do you see the glorious
sparkle of life found
in the earliest
crest of morning?

Seeding, blazing,
blooming, buzzing
singing, growing life?

Oh the canyon emptiness
of your soul if not.
Come please
out into the morning
fill your cup with me.

A little living

One day I decided
I must to do
a little living

no tiptoeing
into the shoreline timidly
but cliff diving in Acapulco

pulling in daring air
toes to the edge
determined to fly fearlessly

leaping
outward into life
leaping

just for a second
gravity forgives
and one lives... yes lives

splashing within
depths consumed anew
popping to the surface

I breath full
having done
a little living

Soft prayers

This morning
it's soft prayers

maybe a word or two
spoken just above silence

these are my favorite prayers
whispered to God

whom I believe listens
more intently

when I live my life
not yelling at myself

The smolder of a woman

She floated,
no flitted
into the room
with her girlish ways

carrying her soft
flowing with her
full of whimsical
dancing charm

Suddenly she's aware
of my eyes upon her body
and the unintentional
sweet fire she's ignited

like the first cords
of a symphony in a quiet hall
the silence vanquished
and her music plays

I move to touch
the hem of her dress
deeply
looking up at her

with that loaded smile
and all of her feminine ways
has become
the smolder of a woman

Back of a yellow taxi

The smelly driver
surveyed the traffic
to find the maximum
wait time to increase
his profits

I watched the meter
ticking away from the
back of a yellow taxi
wondering how I'd
allowed other's to
drive my life

around and around
this dirty garish city
of cavernous shadows
and non seen souls
malcontent

I tapped on the glass
and spoke
I think I'll get out here
Are you sure? he ask
Yes, I do believe
I am sure

Dig down champion

Dig down champion
the day has come
the odds roll
against you

It's the years of
early mornings
mountains climbed
and rivers of pain
you have crossed
that have brought you
to this moment
of mighty trial

Dig down champion

Where the roots hold you
this holiest of places
where your heartbeat begins

Find heart strongly
bring your body to play
your minds edge
to glisten sharply

Pour out your burning spirit
breath it rare
hammers pounding effort

for this is where it exist

The essence of you
your fearlessness
your determination
your spirit

Dig down champion

For many never touch this
few ever challenge themselves
even less actually know
this heart

Dig down champion

Win the day!

Oh spring

We celebrate
fresh beginnings

today we plant
new tiny seeds

we begin pulling up
stubborn old weeds

we go outside
to breath in this air

to rub sunshine
upon our pale faces

this day believing again
in the sweet prayer

whispered softly
oh spring!

Our Bodies

They ask me "Master, speak to us of our bodies."
And I spoke:

See the mighty mountains,
are not the minerals contained
in them found within you?

Feel the wind,
is not the same oxygen found
there within your lungs?

Hear the water,
you understand you are more water than
anything else... Yes?

Every molecule of you,
down to the atom
is the same as the earth,
the wind and water.

How is it you have lost
the truth of this fact?

Your body is meant to be strong
as stone. Cut and smooth alike.
Rising up in grandeur.
Standing bold like the Himalayas.

Your foundation to build upon.
A stone for the artist's hand to shape.

Your body holds the spirit of the winds.
Life itself is dependent
and as fragile as your last breath.
The wind's spirit moves freely
over the entire earth.

It is so for you as well
within your body.

Is it not possible for you to go anywhere on
this planet as your brother the wind does?
As long as you are breathing your body
moves.

And your body of sweet water,
do you not feel the flow of it
in your veins?

The fluid of your hearts very rhythm?
Can you not see the path
your water has cut in this life?

From the sky to the snowy mountain peaks,
melting and moving, carving its holy path?

Your mighty river brings life, and quenches
the thirst of the many.

How have you become so unaware
of the splendor of your own body?

Why do you daily ridicule
and rail so against it?

Please stop!

Never speak against your own body
or the body of another.
You speak of the temple of God.

You must again fall deeply
in love with your body.

Hold it like a lover in the night.
Softly with reverence.
Calmly with compassion.
Fiery with commitment.

For you are your own earth.
You are the free wind blowing.
You contain the vastness of the seas.

Now you know this truth,
please never forget it...
ever.

Forgetting

The dust
has slowly
silently
settled

upon the books
that rest
there on my
wooden shelf

reserved for
the tomes I love
yet no longer
reach for

so strange
how the truest words
that spoke to me of
love, love and more love

now with time
stand wedged
in forgotten
silence

Believe

She ask me of God...
"Do you believe?
for I've never seen him
nor heard his voice."

I ask...
Do you think
God is a keeper
of secrets from you?

invisible he may be,
yet I see his holiness
everywhere
I choose to look

and his voice...
it's a tune that plays
in continuum in my ears

it is I who wonder,
how is it that
you can't see him clear
or hear the sweet songs?

for can
half-hearted
faith even exist?

for the bird flies
or lays dead
upon the dirt

for the river flows
or it is dammed
upstream

and the sea,
she is salty
forever

and the stars,
have always danced
with the moon

my heart knows
sees and hears
and yes... believes

Like silver in the sunlight

Dance
like silver
in the sunlight

spin spin spin
light heeled
dreamer

your soft hair
falling in front
of your gentle face

your very happiness
twisting and shaking
outward from your body

you make me laugh
like silver
in the sunlight

Last three horses

Trinity in a field
they walked together
old friends or lovers
with such slight effort
over the short winter grass

mains tasseled
flowing in the soft air
as the sun pearled
upon their coats of rust
black and brown

did they notice me
a gangly stranger
on their land
a lone seeking observer
lost in the morning

oh they could run
and rule this world
stampede charging the light itself
still they chose to
peacefully amble instead

the holy trinity
strolled with the day
simply being horses
under the blue span

going somewhere unknown

straddling reality
and the thrones of heaven
they know, they see, they are
the last three horses
sceptered and crowned

All that whistles

I have noticed
in my wooded walks
that some birds sing

the same song
note by note
as if calling

calling, calling, calling
for another's song
sweet echo

still other birds sing
with unfastened abandon
flowing melodies pure

alive with the day
rapid and bright
splendiferously

here in my winter woods
cold wind is all that whistles
gone is summers sweet song

yet I remember spring
present in my ear
a song will come again

hands in pockets
with a warm glance skyward
homeward I go

Wintry Walk

I walk alone
on the gray beach
vacant of noisy tourist
and oily sunbathers

for only the purest
venture fort in blustery winter
to dance lovingly
with the wind and water

a lone surfer with his wave
an elderly woman with her dog
and me with my foot prints
falling behind me

the grays and the blues
come together softly
for there is no civil war
between the sky and sea

I noticed the desolation
of thousands of tiny homes
lying in ruin at my feet
beautifully

with thoughts of the sea creatures
long gone
from their protective shells

rolling into simple sand

the cold is beginning
cut upon my ears
and shake my hand
just a bit too briskly

just a wintry walk
to end my day
I think I'll head back
to my own warm shell now

Skin

I know
what rainbows
feel like

Because
I've touched
your skin

The Good Teacher

This morning I see
The Good Teacher
is always teaching

always

It is me
the restless student
who resist the learning

fidgeting in my seat
doodling on life's paper
throwing spit balls across the room

The Good Teacher says:
be calm...
be still...
be quiet... listen

oh how I fight with
my burning ears
hearing such simple words

I realize it is I
who must be ready
for the learning

I must reach out

from the inside
as energy follows attention

for The Good Teacher
is always teaching
always

It is I that must
be willing
to learn

A birds fall

Summer's sweet
branch sitting gone
tomorrow you'll fly south
with the rusting dawn

I've marrow known
that you'd fly away
to warmer weather
and a much sunnier day

just like the others
who've protected their hearts
from winters cold blast
somber our days couldn't last

for I know a little about this life
with it's ever briefer seasons
and long winding reasons
it's clear heart's song

and how one can not change
ones feathers,
only the direction you choose
to fly with them

I'll watch you go
aloft in the morning sky
alone again on the ground

in a bird's fall

5 and 50

I am 5 and 50
the hair on my head
has decided to fly south
and my eyebrows
have decided to grow north

my electric razors buzz
emptied into the sink
has more salt
than pepper now

logs burns slowly
here in my warm hearth
yet sometimes I long for
the raging wildfire of my youth

I miss dancing
and wondering abandon
the unexpected turns
in the rivers' rapid

sweet passions' burn
life's soulful drink
fine wine held tenderly
savored softly

still these winter days
hold riches

glories gold old
memories

laugher real
like warm sweaters
verses in songs
of distant days

I'm 5 and 50
a child's wonder
with a man's heart
I pray I can hang on
to both

Finding her

If you wake up
finding her next to you
her body sleeping warm

If you listen
finding her quiet breathing
stirring your soul

If you reach out
finding her textures soft
arousing your thoughts

If you laugh
finding her waking sounds
more than cute... downright sexy

If you kiss her
finding powerful tenderness
in something so simple

If you envelope her
finding strength in arms
you didn't know you possessed

If you make love to her
finding peace and restoration
next to burning passion

If you look in her eyes
finding a depth of love
unknown to you

If you realize in your spirit
finding her
opens every door in your life

Love this woman

Beyond Myself

I find the need to read
some poignant words
some prose or poetry

to lift my heart
and move me
beyond myself

to see this world
through another's eyes
listen to another's
calling heart

to settle in
like a warm bowl of soup
on a blusterous winters day
soothing

allowing the words
to rest in my belly
and warm my being

to rapturously disappear
into sentences
of nature's ways
of love's flowing
and of rare passion

dog ear'd pages
turning me slowly
in new directions
filling my glass
with new wine

Sing!

Winged friend
with your bright
morning song
of promise

Sing!

Survey the sky
with your chin up
chest out
of confidence

Sing!

Sun cascading
with light upon your wings
warm beams
on this day

Sing!

Fly free
with my soul
lifted high
from your song

Sing!

Green

I believe green
is Gods color
of forgiveness

why else would there
be such an abundance
of it on this earth

emerald understanding blowing
leaves of forgiveness in the wind
soft sprigs of it under my crushing sinful feet

peaceful renewal of green
forgiving the burn of winter
ivy overtaking old walls

that I might hide deeply
green within my soul
growing in forgiveness always

Last blooms

This morning I walk
in silent contemplation
of the simple lives
of my slowly diminishing flowering friends

they came bursting
in spring like fireworks
from the winters' night sky

only to stand boldly
in the summer
like the pedestal sermon
of a fiery Preacher

Holy, Holy, Holy
sweet surrender
followed by tender
redemption

gloriously you've been home
to the crawling creatures
and a soft resting place for
the bee and butterfly

here in the triumph of autumn
these last blooms pose
in the crest of my morning

oh how my heart rejoices
for having actually
known them
by face and by name

embracing the rich color
of their hearts
relishing like a lover
the place they've
found in mine

Gently in the rolling

How is it you've lived your life
wading in the shallows

existing without venturing
beyond the breakers

never losing toe touch
of the bottom

for its here
where the magic is found

to be caught up
gently in the rolling

lifted lightly with the tide
buoyantly floating

come my friend
move with me into the deep

swim with the mermaids
and be weightlessly free

A moment

Strange
how in a moment
you can become
so aware
of all the beauty
you possess

Now you must decide
what to do with it.

Just a bit freer

Out into the morning
of a razor blue sky
I saddle her up
for I need to be out

together we ride
covering distance
breathing the same
sweet air

I feel her beneath me
her need to run
wild so free
I let go of the reins

oh she runs
hard and fast
pure power free
she carries me

to laughter
adrenaline's rush
of nectarous speed
I drink

back to a gallop
having knocked
the dust off our souls

we move toward
the distant horizon
just a bit freer

I was ecstatic

My teacher
laid the bright
construction paper
down upon my desk

oh the mighty colors
orange, purple
yellow and red
with rounded scissors

then my very own
bottle of sticky white
Elmer's glue
smiling

she simply said
the powerful
words of potential...
Create art!

and for the first time
in my tiny, little
young life
I was ecstatic

Glory

To awaken slowly
here amongst the
sauntering clouds
and standing trees

all natures creatures
are reverent
with only the continuous choirs
of distant crickets fills this soft air

the birds are sleeping silent
here before the sun cracks
over the ridge line
blue and distant

I stay quiet myself
allowing the morning
into my soul
compelling my spirit to smile

Glory.

This spinning earth

Sunlight upon your feathers
winged laughing
so high above
this spinning earth

Looking down upon time
it's no wonder you sing
so brightly above
this spinning earth

Perched softly on my feeder
eating your seedy breakfast
so fully above
this spinning earth

Regal cardinal red
fly away into the day
so deliberately above
this spinning earth

White

There is a still beauty
held closely pure
in the white

in the snowy mountain
peaked white
crested against the sky

an innocent flower bloom
its white softness full
in the dawns light

the tearful bride
clothed in her white
dress of the day

a tender white blanket
wrapped snugly around
a slumbering new born

cottony characters
floating white clouds
aloft in your day dreams

the bright white locks
of the saintly grandmother
curled about her face

and the white showing
up more frequently
in my beard as I age wisely

these are my reasons
I keep white so
close to my heart

Exhaling love

The good Lord
gave me a flower
of sweet fragrance

to fill my lungs
with its gentle
glorious aroma

so that I may
find simple
gratefulness

as easily
as taking a breath
and exhaling love

Everything.

The Lord laughed hardly
saying "Oh my child...
you think you know of splendor?

I'll reveal to you
a promise of splendor
unimaginable

Just a breaths whisper
just for joy
just for peace
just for love's sake

That you will see
and know without shadow
that my heart
is truly in everything.

Everything.

To Steal

Doubt is a wicked thief
who sneaks stealthy
into your house
in broad daylight

whose sortie is
to steal
your most prized
possessions;

honest trust and hope pure
the hearths fire of
your burning ambition
and lastly real love

leaving behind shambles
of slow rust
to devour what's left
of your iron heart.

Treasure

Everyday I remind myself:

"I'm an adventurer,
looking for treasure."

Web of diligence

Sitting center
of your structural
billowing sail of capture

You rest upon the hours
of knitting and spinning
the finest of lines

Stealthy balanced awaiting
the non-observant fly
or the lopping bee

I cannot bare to watch
the snaring of death
that adds to your life

Yet I respect
your web of diligence
here in the morning light

Found just before dawn

There is a light
found just before dawn
a place of night fading
with an other worldly feel

where the possibility
and the promise
of the day arrives
in the form of dew

collecting upon everything
in this garden
upon the quick green
and the slow brown

a wet purpose of renewal
resting so pure
the magic of it
is never lost on me

for my heart knows
of renewal
of promise and possibly
found just before dawn

Your sea

Every morning
I feel that I'm standing
at lands end
with my toes
wet at the ocean of you

and all I want to do
all I ever want to do
is dive in
to swim your sea

The wind and the river horse

I ambled at dawn
to the rolling river
to walk her banks
to feel my soul move
gently

only to come upon
a grand calico horse
drinking in softly
his morning reflection
with a reverently bowed head

swiftly upward
his face to the day
he began
a personal conversation
with the wind

they spoke as old friends
at a familiar haunt
with eye caught looks
a flowing of days
spent wild and free

crouching back
on my haunches
holding still my breath
to eavesdrop on their

sweet low conversation

oh how the wind chose
her words tenderly
how magnificently he listened
to her wistfully winding tale
spellbound

the river and the reeds
leafs and branches
listened deeply as well
her story touched my face
and ran through my hair

laughingly the horse
sauntered away southward
the wind whooshed westward
the river ran to the east
and me... I headed northward
into the day

Red Balloon

Ahhh the music
tiny in my ear buds

reaches that moody place of sadness
deep the magical ways of a song

a sweet memory, an emotion tied to my soul
like a red helium balloon

that wiggles and dances
in the wind of my mind

tugging at the heart string
held tightly in my hand

red balloon
I could never let you go

Tonight I fly

Something is magical
aloft between heaven
and earth

Above the dots of light
and the highways of movement

The clouds
beneath my feet
life a slow motion progression
out my tiny window

Distance becomes
a new thing
more horizontal,
more vast

It turns me inward
with thoughts,
words and prayers
with God's view

The blackness of rural country below
and the canopy of stars
pulls me upward gazing

I let my spirit soar
with miracle and wonder

like a child's first everything

Blessed to still be able
to touch this place
in my soul

tonight I fly

Wind

Let me tell you
a secret
that most never learn

That the wind has a heart

A delicate heart
that beats between
lofty heavens
and rocky earth

She whispers stories
about her a long term relationship
with the stars

While she gently turns
the pages of the book
upon my table

She shakes
the emerald leafs cool
in the baking day

I listen to her heartbeat
resting close
to her breast of time
oh wonderful curvy time

EPILOGUE

This book came easier to me than my last two books of poetry. Was it age, more time or more peace? Who knows from where the divine wind blows.

I do know my heart is more open now. I know more love and that's been helpful. I'm no longer tethered by old fears or robbing self doubt.

When the wind blows I catch it in my sails, with my kite or in my hair (what's left of it). I've learned life is more about greater movement. Sweet, slow, graceful movement.

Like the spiral of a grand hawk overhead, looking for a lift from the wind.

Peace
Peace
Peace

Tim 2 Taylor

About the author

Tim 2 Taylor, was a child of the 60's growing up in the slow paced, redneck turbulent south on the outskirts of Atlanta, Georgia. He struggled through the school years as he suffered with undiagnosed dyslexia. A teenage girlfriend gave him his first book of poetry *"The Prophet"* by Kahlil Gibran, which awakened a passion for writing. After graduating, he married his junior high school sweetheart and moved to Florida. Sadly, the marriage ended two years later.

As an adult, Taylor remarried and started a career in advertising. He worked at several nationally ranked agencies as an art director and creative director. Taylor opened his own successful agency 23 years ago -Taylor Productions Inc. He recently launched his second company - Fat As My Dad, LLC.

At the age of 45, Taylor flat lined in the back of an ambulance. Having a near death experience only to be revived, he got a second chance at life. Hence the "2" in his name representing the "2nd " life he's living now.

Within a year he lost 99 pounds and was selected USA Today's 2007 Weight-loss champion and reshaped his life forever.

Currently Tim 2 is a nationally recognized motivational health and fitness speaker and life coach, featured in magazines, radio and TV shows. He is the author of the fitness and weight loss book "Fat As My Dad."

In recent years Tim 2 has rediscovered his passion for writing poetry. He's written two other books of poetry: "The Found Poet - summer and The Found Poet - winter.

Taylor is happily married and is a dedicated father to his beautiful daughter.

www.thefoundpoet.com • #tim2taylor

Please write a review

If you enjoyed this book please be sure to write a five star review at Amazon.com. In today's book selling marketplace reviews are so important. I really love hearing what people think about my work and by writing a review you can let your voice be heard.

Thanks in advance!

Follow me on Facebook
Tim Taylor
and
Tim 2 Taylor

www.ingramcontent.com/pod-product-compliance
Lightning Source LLC
Chambersburg PA
CBHW030509100426
42813CB00002B/405